To Ellie
I'm sure this 'll be you and Simon!
love

Jamie

24/8/03

ANCHOR
BOOKS

LIVING LIFE

Edited by

Sarah Marshall

First published in Great Britain in 2003 by
ANCHOR BOOKS
Remus House,
Coltsfoot Drive,
Peterborough, PE2 9JX
Telephone (01733) 898102

HB ISBN 1 84418 164 2
SB ISBN 1 84418 165 0

FOREWORD

Anchor Books is a small press, established in 1992, with the aim of promoting readable poetry to as wide an audience as possible.

We hope to establish an outlet for writers of poetry who may have struggled to see their work in print.

The poems presented here have been selected from many entries, and as always editing proved to be a difficult task.

I trust this selection will delight and please the authors and all those who enjoy reading poetry.

Sarah Marshall
Editor

CONTENTS

Hospital Nights - 1999	Florence Holland	1
A Friend In Need	Douglas Bryan Kennett	2
Rejection	Steffen Ap Lloyd	4
Strangers	Paul Reynolds	6
A Gypsy Lament	Geo Zori-astro	7
It's All In Today's News	Joy Macdonald	8
Cowes	Pat Williams	9
The Dolphin's Tale	William Thirkettle	10
Dream Maker	S T Vaughan	11
Chapel Street	Janet Eves	12
Why?	Noeleen Tweed	14
The Cow Is Calving	Olive Torkington	15
Within Me	Arthur Thynne	16
Our Special Time	D Plummer	17
Carnival Away Day	Gary Pike	18
I Wandered	Steve Elson	19
Callum And Ryan	Cassie Evans	20
Mills	Shirley Joy Dean	21
Just Walking In The Rain	Sarah Robinson	22
Hymn	Barry Tebb	23
Better Place	Burgess J Barrow	24
The Ability To Understand	Denise Shaw	25
Helping Hands	Karen Stephens	26
Earth's Child	J L Copestake	27
Farms	Derek Spencer	28
A Stress Free Existence	Nicholas Pearce	29
Don't Despair - Care	S Simmonds	30
Live The Life	Jon Oyster	32
Dreamland	Funmilayo Ojedokun	33
Only Fools And Horses Sestina	Mick Nash	34
The Nutcracker	Patricia McQueen	36
The Hopeful Golfer	Kenny McAlpine	38
Angel	J Linehan	39
My England	Alfred John Lawrence	40
Heaven Sent	Donna Kane	41
Recycling	Celia Law	42

Modern Living	Helen Johnson	44
The World We Live In	Barbara Jermyn	45
Noise Pollution	Wendy Ann Jackson	46
I'm Okay, How Are You?	Austin Healey	47
The Light Of Time	Bruce Ing	48
Holidays At Hendaye	Fran Harris	50
Reflections	Joyce Hammond	51
Santa Claus	Tom Clarke	52
Where We Live (You And Me)	Clive Bowen	54
Devil's Bridge, Kirby, Lonsdale	Albert E Bird	55
Pokipan	Lucy Fell	56
Sad, Sad World	William J Bartram	57
Help!	E Balmain	58
Little Me	Maureen Arnold	59
Carpe Diem	John Andrews	60
Untitled	Philip Allen	61
'Anging In The Shed	James Allen	62
A Theory Of Belief	David C Christopher	63
Stabs In The Dark	Tim Frogman	64
Baby Bliss	Nick Clifton	65
Daydreams	Beryl Clark	66
Our Rich Life	Valerie Catterall	67
Blackened Tunnel	Linda Chapman	68
Disharmony	Anne Omnibus	70
Our World Today	Betty Greig	71
Bridge	Steven Gunning	72
American Space Tragedy	Jocky	73
Mother Nature	Don Friar	74
She's Calling From Within	Sue Elle	75
Two Paintings	Norman Bissett	76
Sleep Sabotage	Joyce Atkinson	77
A Little Humour	Keith L Powell	78
Know Each Other	Tom Usher	79
Anguish	Pat Hunter	80
Saving The Planet	Fiona Louise Watson	81
Time	Christine Mitchell	82
Friend On Drugs	Dawn Wylie	83
Ultimate Aim	Louise Davies	84

The Race	Clare Todd	85
True Friendship	Joyce Stokes	86
When Your Ship Comes In	Leslie Frank Checkley	87
T' New Year	Mandy M McKee	88
I Am Waiting	Carol Boneham	89
I'm On My Own	Kirsty Wing	90
The Young Of Today	Margaret McIlwaine	91
Birthdays	Jill Corkish	92
Untitled	Jenny Mill	93
Awakening	Robert McGarry	94
Sailing	Christopher F Morris	95
The Evening Class	Joy Lewis	96
The Mermaid And		
The Troubadour	Patrick Lyseight	98
A Spider's Tale	Jean Marguerite Dangerfield	99
The Turn Of The Card	Beryl Powles	100
Essential And Precious	Christine Frederick	101
Education Plus	Lionel J Nokes	102
The Ties That Bind	Jo-Ann Waldron-Hall	103
Mammo	Carlie Morgans	104
Goodbye	B Green	105

HOSPITAL NIGHTS - 1999

Lying on a bed of pain
Listening, watching, hurtling rain,
Lights are out and patients sleep
As nurses, tireless watch do keep.

Outside, cars go rattling by
Now and then, a shrill sharp cry,
Patients wake and look around
Worried, and wondering at the sound.

Sirens blare, and voices shout,
So we ask, 'What's it about?'
Suddenly, all is very still
No more do cars and voices shrill.

Gradually patients go to sleep
Lulled by the sound of snoring deep,
Lights go on, we wake again
To the sounds of morning and pouring rain.

Florence Holland

A FRIEND IN NEED

The house was sold, so now no base
As distant oceans we embrace.
'Good luck!' 'God's speed!', is what they say
As breezes sail our yacht away.

It took but just 1,000 miles
Before concern replaced our smiles.
The surgeon's task we thought was done,
So why do serious symptoms come?

In street-side phone the coins clatter,
Car horns blare and people chatter,
Hard to hear and hard to speak,
Will the outlook be that bleak?

No friends within 100 miles
Of where the surgeons want their trials,
Once again to cut and see,
Producing joy, or misery.

No word nor card for several years
Between two men who had been peers
Within a company's cut and thrust -
But twixt the two respect and trust.

The phone was answered as though had been
We'd never left that working scene.
'Sorry to hear,' 'Come stay with us,'
Welcome words - no hint of fuss.

Depressed to airport, train and cab,
From sun to England looking drab,
And then at last at journey's end,
One time colleague becomes good friend.

A bed, a base, a home, a car,
Recovering slowly from the scar.
His wife and he so generously
Showed what in life true friendship be.

Douglas Bryan Kennett

REJECTION

A man all alone with a broken heart,
is a man all alone and torn apart,
walking alone with a shuffling stride,
and from this world his pain does hide,
for a man alone with a broken heart,
walks with no one by his side.

A man alone with a broken heart,
hides the pain of all his world,
a pain so great he tears apart,
and his heart it all unfolds.
To God he cries and God alone,
he cries for mercy so,
for the pain inside becomes so great,
he starts to lose control.

A man alone with a broken heart,
is a man without a friend,
no woman to hold just split apart,
nothing to hold no soul or heart.
An empty vessel is all that's left,
his mind in turmoil and his life in a mess,
no children to see or children to hold,
no Xmas together or stories to be told.

A man alone with a broken heart,
is a man who plays the part,
his head held high a smile on his face,
walking alone amongst the whole human race,
living alone and sat in his cell,
no one to talk to and living a hell,
crying for help and all on deaf ears,
sat all alone and drowning in tears.

A man all alone with a broken heart,
must fight for himself and find a new start,
find a new life and find a new heart,
to mix with the crowd and again play the part,
help me Lord he cries once again,
to give him the strength and heal all his pain,
and to grant him his wish to start all again.

To go into the world upright and alone,
to find a new woman and make a new home,
one day he will find her that is a fact,
their eyes will meet and they'll form a pact,
the love they will form will be from Heaven above,
a bond made in Heaven and so full of love,
but his barriers are up for his own protection,
because God didn't teach man
How to handle rejection.

Steffen Ap Lloyd

STRANGERS

Two strangers standing in a crowded room
Eyes watching for secret glances,
Straining to see through the smoky gloom,
Fearful of missing the smallest of chances.

Will they find love in this place?
Is their future here for all to see?
They search for acknowledgement on any face,
A look that says, you and me.

People throng and mill around
Hypocritical smiles and forced laughter,
For the strangers to win
They must hold their ground,
Or forfeit the battle forever after.

But now the party's ending
Guess it wasn't meant to be,
Time to close the file, 'romance pending'
Another failed attempt, time to flee.

They step out into the rainy night
Their moods, like the weather, dull and drab,
Then, in the hazy glow of the street light
Their eyes meet, they smile
'Shall we share a cab?'

Paul Reynolds

A GYPSY LAMENT

(This poem is primarily dedicated to Dotun Adebayo,
Whose African gypsy-friendly attitude, inspired me
To create it - on the 'Lambeth Readers Day' 22/2/03)

Look at me and see! I am neither black, brown or white!
Am I different if I prefer peace to war, day to night?
Or, when I hate darkness of death and love the light.
So please, someone tell me, am I wrong or am I right?

And being a Satanised and worse, Serbian gypsy-man,
Always hated and persecuted by every 'blond Aryan',
Is by far worse now, and ever, than being a Jew!
Especially, because we are poor, and we are few.

Nobody mentions our 'holocaust'; which one is our land.
Go back to Egypt gypsy! What to do, and where to stand?
We have no power, no lawyers - justice for us to demand.
We sing - our songs are sad, but have not a single band.

Yet, they say, God is just, and Jesus died for us all!
Jehovah has his people, but for us there isn't a soul.
For, we are neither black, brown or master race white,
They always say we are wrong, even when we are right.

Geo Zori-astro

It's All In Today's News

I wake up every morning eagerly awaiting today's news
Desperate to read all the different views
Of vandals and criminals and some charged with rape
Drunk drivers, drug users and some by loopholes who escape

Scan the new hatches and admire the new matches
Then glean every detail of the recent despatches
Thrive on people's downfalls feeling rather sadistic
As if we were trained as some superior life critic

No news of anyone just enjoying their job
Or happy and content to being earning a few bob
They dictate to the nation how not to punish a child
Then wonder why some young folk often go wild

Can't anyone see that it's really quite cruel
Not knowing in this life they have to follow the rule
The best way to learn is to be shown by example
Our derogatory media display is such a bad sample

Maybe we should clean up our act and show them the way
So that we can be proud of the next generation someday
Study the world's nations where they are nearly free from crime
And within an acceptance regime brings ours into line.

Joy Macdonald

COWES

The Regatta was drawing to a close
And we joined the crowd for the firework show
What stunning colours reaching high
Exploding sparkle across the sky

A hundred or so spectator craft
With their tiny lights fore and aft
Like floating lamps reflect the scene
Seemed like a picture from a dream

Next day we saw some final races
Watching those crews go through their paces
Many times the gun gave a blast
Redwings, X Boats and Contessa Class

Later the Sigmas appear from the west
Changing sails to get the best
Those billowing spinnakers reaching for the line
Which of these will make the best time?

Lots of boats jiggling around, so hard to see through
We can just see *Orange*, *Kingfisher* and *Maiden* too
And then we spot Ellen MacArthur sail her little *Corabie*
That left us all with a great memory.

Pat Williams

THE DOLPHIN'S TALE

The night was dark, the wind was cold
As this tale of heroism begins to unfold.
A crew of sailors helplessly lost
On a vast, wide ocean with waves rising high,
The whole of the ship covered over with frost
They're hoping for help, with the hint of a sigh
Someone to help them, deliverance at no cost.

With the sea growing rougher,
Their plight getting tougher,
The men spied a dolphin swimming around
Their ship, which was heaving.
They stood there disbelieving
Through eyes really craving,
That at last they'd finally been found.

The life saving dolphin swam close by the ship,
But the terrified sailors weren't just on a trip.
They'd set out to deliver a cargo of gold
Then the sea finally beat them, they found it so cold.
With pleading, wide eyes, they urged dolphin on,
But then, in a flash, the dolphin had gone.
Away to get help, the crew thought they were done.

Then back came the dolphin, with helpers galore,
A sight which the ailing crew'd never seen before.
Was the dolphin really going to help them?
If they had ever seen a saviour, this dolphin was a gem.
At once, the sailors who'd come to save them
Took the stranded crew aboard the other ship,
They were grateful of the dolphin's merciful trip.

William Thirkettle

DREAM MAKER

Little man, with funny feet
Bowler hat and baggy seat
Bendy stick, all fall down
Charlie Chaplin, wears the crown.

Stan and Ollie, double up
Pickfords, drink from loving cup
Buster Keaton, keystone cop
W C still the top.

West and Harlow, wink the eye
Valentino, makes them sigh
Silent horror, with no scream
Hollywood magic, sells the dream.

Laughter maker, wartime tale
Sweet romance, men from jail
English, Yank, some from France
Lively music, makes them dance.

Moviola brings a tear,
Sometimes fun, then it's fear
Camera rolls, dream makers
Behind the glitter, money takers.

On the screen, a laughing face
At the bar, all heartache
Plastic kisses, on the screen
Lonely girl, a movie queen.

S T Vaughan

CHAPEL STREET

I've been thinking of when, we lived in Chapel Street,
Times were hard then, and a job to make ends meet.
You didn't have a washing machine, to help you get through,
Just a copper and a mangle, the rest was down to you.
When I came home from school, the wireless would be on,
A lovely smell of polish, and everything just shone.
If we played you up at all, you'd give us a clout,
Then if things got out of hand, you would always shout,
'Wait till your dad gets home, he'll give you what for,'
We knew you wouldn't tell him, well you never had before.
We often went out with Alice and Grace,
Sometimes we went down the wood,
And on the way back took a short cut,
Across Hounslow's Field' if we could.
He'd holler and shout if he saw us, and send us back down the lane,
I'm sure he knew when his back was turned, that we would try again.
When I came in the house one day, everything had changed,
There was no music while you work, and the furniture re-arranged.
In fact it wasn't ours at all, and as I ran out the door,
I knew I shouldn't be there, we'd moved two days before.
We moved to number 24, where everything was new,
We didn't need the tin bath, and we had an inside loo.
There's so much I remember, of our days in Chapel Street,
Like the times when we were really cold, or didn't have enough to eat.
But most of the memories are happy, cos we really had lots of fun,
And we got on well with the neighbours, that is except for one.
Nobody liked Miss Thomkins, she always made such a fuss,
And I don't think she liked children, well I know she didn't like us.
She said she'd lock us in her cellar,
If she caught us scrumping from her trees,
She always seemed so creepy, I made sure she didn't catch me.

A lot has happened since those days,
The family has grown and we've gone our separate ways,
But wherever we go and whatever we do,
We always come back Mum, just to see you.

Janet Eves

WHY?

How am I going to cope,
How am I going to get by,
Not knowing if you're going to live,
Not knowing if you're going to die?
Why did they make you do this?
Why did they take you away?
Can anyone answer these questions
That I think of every hour of the day?

What made you join?
What made you go,
Could you not have got a different job
With friends instead of foes?
You wouldn't have to worry or be careful where you go,
Because you'd be safe at home with the people that you know.

Maybe I'm being selfish,
Maybe I'm being cruel,
But I can't help the way I feel,
Even if I am being a fool.
If anyone can answer my questions, it's the big man up above,
I am only getting to know you,
So if I lose you now, I lose my love.

Noeleen Tweed

THE COW IS CALVING

The cow is calving, hurry they said,
We don't want either one to be dead.
Her sides were heaving, she was moaning as well,
Stamping her feet, she must be in hell.
Quick, its head is coming out,
It must be a big one by the size of its snout.
Grab its foot and pull when she strains,
It can't be helped if she's having pains.
Feel for the calf's legs and attach a rope,
We'll give her a hand to help her to cope.
Carefully now, just pull when she strains,
Its head is appearing, its tongue hanging out
And its big, staring eye is rolling about.
The cow gives a bellow and out comes the calf.
She jumps to her feet, the pain's forgotten
As she licks the calf from top to bottom.
Nature's a wonderful thing if it's not you having the calf.

Olive Torkington

WITHIN ME

When you passed on
Where did you go
Or did you stay,
Within me?

For when I smile
I feel you smile.
I feel your smile
Within me.

And when I laugh
I hear you laugh.
I hear your laugh,
Within me.

But when I cry
I hear you sigh.
'I'm here'
'Right here'
'Within you'.

When you passed on
You didn't go.
You stayed
Right here.

Within me.

Arthur Thynne

OUR SPECIAL TIME

Where we used to snuggle up together,
We lie side by side in companionable silence:
At first we never needed bedside lights or glasses,
We only had eyes for each other:
The exhaustion of children soon put pay to that!
'That' was relegated to birthdays and Christmas,
As a special treat of stolen moments, snatched in-between.

Now we watch television, comfortably propped up in bed,
When a drama or play engage us
Or failing that, we read.

Always for me it's a political thriller,
For you, a historical northern romance,
Sometimes for fun, we swop:
You, are absorbed by 'double agents' and chicanery,
Me, whether the heroine will get her man,
That the hero, even for me as a man, is so unbelievably blind!

Or in reverie, we each ponder on our day
Laughing at the comedy,
Commiserating on the tragedies of daily life.

My love for you has grown stronger with every passing moment,
Your touch or word during a tirade or monologue,
Means the world to me.

It's here we debate our worries and concerns:
At first, even now, it's family and friends.
Invariably your shrewd observation cuts to its heart,
Whilst I flounder in the morass of my emotions
But, on occasions, it is me who gives *you* insight.
Always, this is mine, our, special place
Here, together, with you.

D Plummer

CARNIVAL AWAY DAY

The troupe is all assembled, (a little late it's true;
Our meeting time was one o'clock, and now 'tis half-past two).

Still we've loads of time to get there; no need for any fuss
For, if we don't arrive on cue, they'll surely wait for us.

So off we go then, 'All aboard', the journey we must start.
But, 'Alf a mo, which way to go?' We hadn't thought of that.

Procession starts at 'alf-past three, only fifty miles distant;
Auld 'Arry knows a wee short cut, that'll get us there 'this instant'.

The route agreed, we could proceed but, for further complication,
The music disc somewhere is lost; we must discover its location.

At last it's found ('twas in *'her'* bag, we always knew *'she'* had it!)
So settle down, enjoy the ride, no more can go wrong, *can it?*

Our progress is frustrated by the need to pause en-route
For cigarette consumption, and a cup of tea, to boot.

Finally on-site all gather round, preparations to be made
Kit unpacked and costumes donned; dancers *'formed up'* for parade.

Beset we are with last minute panics: Fred won't dance in the middle;
Billy's skirt keeps slipping down and Ray *(again!)* must 'piddle'!

Now, gingerly our dancers loosen ageing faculties
(Tom's back is sore, Al's shoulder aches and Bert's got dodgy knees).

Alas, too late we're ready, to join the processional train,
Let's 'pack it in' and go back home (at least it didn't rain!).

On the tedious, homeward journey we commiserate and sigh
Regretting this, and earlier days, when life has passed us by.

Gary Pike

I WANDERED

I wandered lonely as a cloud,
wondering where the daffodils were.
I suddenly realised, thinking right out loud,
that we were actually into summer.

I thought the weather had warmed a bit,
looking at my red burned skin.
I remember looking for somewhere to sit,
thinking, what a state I'm in.

I found a place, under the shade
of a great big apple tree.
It felt as if this parasol,
was made only just for me.

An apple fell upon the floor,
reminding me of old schooldays,
and the physics lessons, that were a bore,
with grumpy old Mr Hayes.

I cooled a while and had a chill,
just for a moment or two,
just before, I go back down the hill
to admire the wonderful view.

Steve Elson

CALLUM AND RYAN

Callum and Ryan are boys
Who like to play with toys.
One is two and the other is three
Whom I always look forward to see.

When they grow older what would they be?
One will be a doctor, the other professor of history?
Whatever the future will bring
Their praises I will sing
For my grandsons will always be
One who is two and the other three.

Cassie Evans

MILLS

Grinding the corn to make the bread
That makes sure that we all are fed.
The solitary windmill turns its sail
Through summer sunshine and winter gale.
High on its lofty hillside perch
The wind's direction is its eager search;
And looking down on the marshy ground
It knows where the wind pumps can be found.
Standing in greater numbers at the water's edge.
Where the banks are lined with rushes and sedge;
Their turning sails against the changing sky
Are keeping the waterlogged marshes dry.
The years pass by - artists paint and poets dream
At these long ago masterpieces in life's great scheme.

Shirley Joy Dean

JUST WALKING IN THE RAIN

With a feeling of gladness,
As I stepped off the train.
I started to walk home
And it began to rain!

With a feeling of sadness,
I thought, oh, not again!
I stumbled over stones
In the downpour of rain!

With a feeling of meekness,
As I walked in the rain.
It's rather refreshing,
I'm not in any pain.

With a feeling of wetness,
I trudged along the lane.
Getting wetter and wetter
But enjoying the rain!

With a feeling of goodness,
I was on dry terrain,
I towelled my wet hair
And thought of the rain.

Feeling such wonderness.
Is God crying again?
The heaven just opened,
Our plants can smile again.

With a feeling of boldness,
Flowerheads rise up again
Nature is wonderful:
The sun and of course - rain!

Sarah Robinson

HYMN

How I love the working class girls of Leeds,
Their mile-wide smiles, eyes bright as beads,
Their young breasts bobbing as they run,
Hands quick as darting fish, lithe legs
Bare as they scramble over the Hollows
With brown-soled feet and dimpled bums
Half-covered with knickers, and short frocks
Full of flowers and their delicate ears,
Perfect teeth and flickering tongues, the
Fragile bones of their cheeks, the soft
Sweetness of their soprano voices dying
Away into the unforgotten magenta and
Yellow-ochre of innumerable twilights.

Barry Tebb

BETTER PLACE

The world would be adorned with kindness,
When stark actions become less mindless.
That's when right controls wrong,
To view life path with happy song.

What's this notion of stealth and zeal,
That add no adhesion to the appeal.
The blight produced by cunning greed
Would never nurture from the seed.

The seeds that's planted in the mind,
That sacrifice the blood of humankind.
Because of half truth and deceit,
To gain control, there is no receipt.

Consider the seasons as they glow,
The weather hastens high and low.
In spring the buds and flowers rush,
Awakened from winter's hush.

Burgess J Barrow

THE ABILITY TO UNDERSTAND

You're everything to me, you fully understand,
As a waif as I lay helpless, you took hold of my hand.
The only one with the ability to understand my plight
You took up constant attendance, for me began the fight.

With your hand you did not let go,
You taught me all I needed to know.
My mind was broken in half, in two
I joined a never-ending queue.

And as I queued I began to learn
Your ways and thoughts I did discern.
From nothing I did start to feel
Myself you taught me how to heal.

Denise Shaw

HELPING HANDS

No one saw me crying, no one knew my name,
Which makes me think, I only have myself to blame.
It's my own fault, for getting so involved,
Even before my own problems have been solved.
I try to help others, but myself I then neglect,
Just to prove to myself and others that I have respect;
Care, love and want to understand,
Trying if I can to satisfy a demand.
But I take it all straight to heart,
Then analyse deeply every part.
My mother and father mean the most to me,
Because without them, I wouldn't even be.
Although I find it hard to cope with very much,
With the help from my family and friends caring touch
Kind words and shoulder they lend,
I'm able to get through, with the help of a friend.

Karen Stephens

EARTH'S CHILD

Your bare feet touch the Earth so fair
With each and every timely stride
The soil you squidge beneath your toes
Softening with the season's tides

The sun he glows down on the brow,
Tinting golden the forest's hue,
You spread your wings to feel his touch,
As the winds they race your fingers through.

As you gaze into the water's surface
Your beauty paints your reflection deep
Your peachy cheeks and windswept hair
Mirrored your inner secrets seep

Your bed a browned mass of twigs and leaves
Gathered from last autumn's fall
Comfort you found, underneath the bough
Of the wisest tree of them all

Night-time sheds an unlit curtain
Moonlight shimmering, illuminating the grove
She whispers to you secrets of old
And wraps you tight in her motherly hold

A sacred being of Earthly kin
At one in reverence with nature
They talk to you and keep you safe
You are their spirit son/daughter.

J L Copestake

FARMS

When walking through this pleasant land
In small group or in larger band
One thing that tends to spoil the charm
Is coming across a deserted farm

When thinking back to younger days
A picture comes in through the haze
Of farmers working night and day
Producing meat and fruit and hay

During difficult times of war
When Britain had to close the door
The farmer with his plough that sped
Managed to keep the country fed

And all the thanks the farmers get
For using all that toil and sweat
Is having all their gains denied
And then are told to 'set-aside'

The leaders of this country
Should look into the pantry
And then without any qualms
Should place orders with the farms.

Derek Spencer

A STRESS FREE EXISTENCE

I wish for a life without stress and pain,
No worries of fortune, intentions to gain,
No orders and commands taking control of your life,
No concerns of colleagues turning the knife,
To be in charge of your destiny, no one else can dictate,
No worries for others, your decisions to make,
No cares about bills or money to pay,
Your future lies ahead, should you cease the day?
A life is for living, you pursued yourself,
A life isn't about just creating a wealth,
A life of fulfillment, not financial gain,
I wish for a life without the stress and pain.

Nicholas Pearce

DON'T DESPAIR - CARE

You know I often wonder what,
When walking down the street,
The problems people face,
The people that I meet.

I know we think we've got it tough,
I know that things are hard,
And sometimes it can be so difficult,
To go that extra yard.

The bills get high, the kids play up,
Your partner's little help,
It's easy then to have a moan,
At the hand that we've been dealt.

Our little world of aches and pains,
And trivial little sores,
So easy then to pass the buck,
Adding blame to the cause.

I've been there and know it's true,
Done all these things I've said,
But at least when all is said and done,
I can still sleep within a bed.

Now I'm sitting here, it's raining hard,
Windy and cold beyond belief,
Whilst way out there beyond my sight,
For some there's no relief.

No food, no clothes, no warmth, no bed,
No love, no care, no help.
They're lying in a gutter,
As rats pick at their scalp.

Women too scared to say a word,
They'll make their husband sore,
The food's not right, the house unclean,
Their face smashed in a door.

Children too who've never known,
The feeling of being loved,
On Christmas Day the only gift,
A fist that wears a glove.

Young kids so high, they need a fix,
They've no hope of finding work,
They prowl our streets in little gangs,
For people they can hurt.

Business shut down, men unemployed,
Women are forced to the street.
These are shadows that pass us by,
Ghosts that we never meet.

Don't get me wrong and don't misunderstand,
I'm not saying your problems are few,
Just be aware that when things seem real bad,
There's always someone who is worse off than you.

S Simmonds

LIVE THE LIFE

Live the life of a poet.
See personal hygiene as the conspiracy
It really is.
Go to pubs and don't buy drinks.
Know that what you say is absolutely right,
It's just that no one gets it yet.
Have meaningless sex,
Lamenting throughout on loneliness.
Don't go anywhere unless you are going to perform.
Smoke cigarettes always.
Resign yourself to poverty, conflict and insomnia
With open arms.
Find greater meaning in chewing gum.
Never, ever, ever, ever, ever read poetry.

Jon Oyster

DREAMLAND

Lay down your head
On your soft cradle bed
For now the day must end
As you nod off to dreamland

You dream of fields of flowers
And everything that showers
You dream of laughing streams
As you travel in the land of dreams

Over hill and over plain
To a land where only you reign
To a land where people call your name
A land of glory and fame

Funmilayo Ojedokun

ONLY FOOLS AND HORSES SESTINA

The long plonker Rodney and his brother Del,
Just south of the river in Peckham did dwell,
Their old Uncle Albert lived with them as well,
You may think that Peckham's the entrance to Hell,
Del's wife, Raquel, was a talented girl,
Del and Rodney took goods to the market to sell.

One day, at the market, they'd not much to sell,
So Rodney turned round to his big brother Del,
And told him he'd just met a heck of a girl,
In the posh part of London Cassandra did dwell,
He said for her he'd go through the jaws of Hell,
He said he loved her and she loved him as well.

The Trotters felt their lives were going quite well,
With plenty of goods at the market to sell,
In their trade, the bad times could sometimes be hell,
But right now, life was good for both Rodney and Del,
Despite the fact that they in Peckham did dwell,
But each had the love of a wonderful girl.

Each vowed to look after his gem of a girl,
And work hard at business and really do well,
And both move upmarket, somewhere nice to dwell,
So people could then respect Rodney and Del,
They'd no longer live at the entrance to Hell,
Or take hooky gear to the market to sell.

Rodney thought that his nephew had been spawned in Hell,
When Damian was born to Del's wonderful girl,
Raquel felt they'd both been blessed, as also did Del,
Uncle Albert was chuffed with young Damian as well,
With a family to keep, much more goods they must sell,
Or else for their whole lives in Peckham they'd dwell.

In Peckham forever they'd no wish to dwell,
It was not far removed from a life spent in Hell,
So more hooky gear Del attempted to sell,
To buy luxuries fit for his son and his girl,
So he worked very hard and he tried to do well,
There was none so determined to succeed as Del.

For Del and his girl to get out of their hell,
He needed to sell and to really do well,
Peckham isn't the place where the best people dwell.

Mick Nash

THE NUTCRACKER

Long ago we had a tiny bust, perched high on mantle shelf,
The image represented Shakespeare, great English bard himself!
We used it as a nutcracker on Hallowe'en night,
And little thought of the famous image on that infamous night.
For Hallowe'en represents spirit world and dead spirits gone forever,
But Shakespeare's spirit in his plays and poems lives on forever.

Shakespeare was born in Stratford-on-Avon 1564 on St George's Day,
He died in 1616 on April 23rd - his 52nd birthday!
Shakespeare had older wife, Anne and three children, only one son.
Hamlet his son died young - which caused him much grief.
His tragic play Hamlet immortalised his son and his life too brief.
Perhaps reversed roles, living prince - dead father gave him some relief.

He studied the Bible, the classics and learned from them.
As actor trained in Globe Theatre, London, he achieved great fame.
He studied writing, then playwright and part owner became.
Attaining popularity with King James who gave his troupe
                                        special name,
The Royal Players, a sign of royal favour, prestige and power.
Now he entertained, enlightened and inspired, over his rivals towered.

His plays re-enacted history, wars, comedies and tragedies combined.
He tells of seven stages in life, with comedy and tragedy outlined.
He wrote 38 plays and 154 sonnets and short poems with
                                        ending couplet.
He learned from history and lives both royals and commoners,
                                        a doublet.
English though changed since his day - its richness continues to present.
Shakespeare added 170 new words, his magic words still live on today.
His life contained many elements, both tragic and happy events.

His plays published in 1623 posthumously - yet mystery
remains unsolved?
Did he work alone or with co-writer? But this riddle can never
be resolved.
For dead men tell no more tales today, their silence forever must keep,
Like Hallowe'en ghosts of yesterday, they must rest in eternal sleep!

Patricia McQueen

THE HOPEFUL GOLFER

You started with spirits high,
Thinking I'm a brilliant kinda guy.
You looked the part with clubs and trolley,
The big let-down was your mum's old brolley!

You had more strokes than a coronary ward,
You put the greenkeeper to the sword.
You wondered why your putts never dropped,
It's cos you're that bad you'd get golf stopped.

You were ultra consistent, bad all day,
Thought you'd get better the more you play.
Bunkers, rough and water, you were in the lot,
The next Tiger Woods, I think not!

All your shots were a slice or hook,
Some were that bad we couldn't look.
You were really awful, all the way round.
122 shots taken, only three in bounds.

But take heed from this and don't despair,
You suited the 'plus fours' you dared to wear.
A fashion statement you did make,
When you drove the buggy into the lake.

But all in all a good day out,
Unless you were a golf ball getting knocked about.
But golf is a game your style is not fitting,
Better start now taking up some knitting.

Kenny McAlpine

ANGEL

I've received my halo
My world is now calm
I am your angel
To guide you from harm

My spirit is free
And so is my soul
Bury my outside shell
In a 6ft hole

Don't wear black
And do not cry
For I am watching out for you
Looking down from a high

Remember me happy
Looking at my best
My spirit lives on
My body's at rest

Celebrate my life
Wipe the tear from your eye
For I am now a star
Shining down from the sky

So family and friends
My love lives on
I am your angel
My spirit's never gone

J Linehan

MY ENGLAND

Where has my England gone, the one I knew as a child?
With streets full of laughter and pleasures untold,
No fear had our parents of traffic and vice,
In spite of the poverty life was quite nice.

When war was declared, we all rather feared,
But with such good friends and neighbours as one
In spite of the Blitz, the battle was won.

When peace was declared and trouble was ended,
We enjoyed the peace we had defended.
But it wasn't to last, this peace so hard fought,
With crime all around us it left us distraught.

With muggings and drugs and break-ins galore,
We even get frightened to open the door.
And now with our life span so near to its end,
We think of the loved ones who died to defend
The England we know.

Where has my England gone?

Alfred John Lawrence

HEAVEN SENT

Heaven hear the gentle echo
feathers fall from the sky
just another happy soul
Children's laughter far and wide

Heaven hold the golden sun
days and nights come and go
fall asleep everyone
Watch your dreams go to and fro

Heaven send the pouring rain
thunder lights up the sky
winds will blow a gale
Hear them in their torment cry.

Donna Kane

RECYCLING

Now the Council, bless them, gave us a bin
And this was to put all our rubbish in
This bin has wheels and is really quite big
It took everything from tins to the odd branch or twig
Now this bin is green and most would tell
Emptied weekly, it seemed to work well

Then came a small bin and that was green too
We then had our rubbish to separate and sort through
In the little one we put cardboard, paper and mags
And in the other one we put rubbish tied up in bags
Our green paper bin was emptied every other week
We were happy to help with the recycling they seek

Then came a bombshell, a brown bin appeared
And the news that came with it our contentment disappeared
The brown bin was for garden rubbish, anything that would rot
But emptied once a fortnight, happy I am not
When you have a compost, you don't have it by the door
The smell and the flies just makes me want to roar

This means the green one is emptied only once a fortnight
High temperatures turned flies into maggots, oh what a sight
Although everything is in bags the smell is diabolical
Why the Council should cause this problem is just illogical
Recycling is a good idea, but it has not been thought through
To have bins emptied once a fortnight, just will not do

This just defeats the object, it just baffles me
Cardboard I once recycled, I now put in my bin, you see
This stops the bags from sticking to the bottom of the bin
And soaks up the stinking liquids that linger within
The newspapers I once saved, I used to wrap everything twice
Because flies and maggots, I do not wish to entice

Then on top of that, I spray the bin with fly spray
Now aerosol cans damage the ozone layer, they say
This means it will get hotter, so our bins will smell more
As it is now, I'm frightened to open my back door
With the smell of rotting grass and two weeks of doggy poo
Come on Tunbridge Wells Council - this really won't do!

Celia Law

MODERN LIVING

Have you noticed something of our lives these days
How things are changing in so many ways?
Square boxes are the controllers for you and me
If you wish to learn the news, check the one called TV

Then we're told there's the one called the computer
Just switch on and shop to order the lot
Then if you should require a little cash in hand
Insert a card in banks' boxes on the wall, for cash on demand

Of course the box on the wall can decide not to pay
And you can't even ask, why not today
You see the person to person touch, has gone away
What happened to the people who used to be there
To exchange a cheery word and ask how you fare?
These boxes all seem so clever and ever so smart
But what matters most is they don't have a heart.

Helen Johnson

THE WORLD WE LIVE IN

She's on the critical list, what does this mean?
Is she too far gone, too ill, too lean?
She has resources and the will to survive
Who has the skill to keep her alive?

Yes, Mother Earth is losing its beauty,
Wicked men scheme and take her booty.
Polluted oceans, bad air to breathe,
We cover our noses with our sleeve.

Little help for education, healthcare or old age,
Or battered families, sadly filled with rage.
Thieves break in, despite alarms and locks,
Whilst we work to keep families from taking knocks.

The media play games with people's lives,
Their sins pile way up to the skies,
Our sons are born to go to war,
While earthly rulers set out to score.

Teenage pregnancies, joy-riding in cars,
Destroys many lives, leaving deep scars.
The muggings, killings, the drugs, and rape,
Destroy faith in humans at such a rate.

Will man's domination of man, ever end?
I'd like to think so, let's all be friends.
Mother Earth is resourceful, she will survive,
Our creator designed her to always revive.

Barbara Jermyn

NOISE POLLUTION

It's that noise again
Is it a supersonic boom?
We can hear it so loud
From our living room.

It could be an earthquake
A blast or a bomb.
It might be an explosion
But I could be quite wrong.

The house is a-rattling
From the awful din,
As it shakes the foundations
And our patience wears thin.

It happens so frequent
It's driving us mad
Oh pass us the earplugs
This really is bad!

So what is it? You ask
That caused this of late.
You'll be shocked when I tell . . .

It's only the passage gate!

Next time you unlock, think of others too:
Please close the gate gently, as you
make your way through.

Don't swing it or slam it, or exert any force,
Just click it in place, as a matter of course.

It really is simple and no effort at all,
It will stop all the bolts coming loose, from the wall!

It will stop us from jumping out of our skin,
When folk need access, to go out or in!

Wendy Ann Jackson

I'M OKAY, HOW ARE YOU?

I'm going to write a poem
And start it at the end
I'll finish with the beginning
Now how is that my friend?

I'm writing this last week you see
So I've got plenty of time
Perhaps by the time I finish it
It will only be a quarter to nine

The time right now is ten o'clock
I think that's what it says
But life is very confusing
In so many ways

Last night was very stormy
But everywhere was dry and clear
A few more minutes to go now
And it will be half-past here

What in the world is wrong with me?
Am I going round the bend?
If the answer's yes, to my question
Why don't you join me, my friend?

Austin Healey

THE LIGHT OF TIME

The diamond mines of Africa are like a living hell,
with heat and noise and smell of fear and lack of trust, as well.
Yet from these pits of darkness come rough pebbles, round and grey,
which, in the hands of craftsmen skilled, will be transformed one day.
Their facets and their colours true will show them in their prime
and after countless ages, they'll reflect the light of time.

The battlefields of anywhere are like a living hell,
with heat and noise and smell of fear and lack of trust, as well.
The playing fields of Eton were said to generate
the leadership and teamwork that would conquer any state.
But the poor lad in the infantry, besmeared with blood and grime,
knew nothing of that mystery we call the light of time.

Of all the subjects taught in school there's one which fails outright.
We never learn from history, we do not see the light.
Each stupid generation, with its politics of greed,
ignores all human misery, uncertainty and need,
repeating the same blunders and committing the same crime:
denial of truth, and blindness to the ancient light of time.

We use our cleverest people to find more routes to death,
To poison and to blast apart and take away the breath.
There's no justification for this folly and this pain,
this waste of men and women we really can't sustain.
There is no cause that's worthy of this lunacy sublime;
this is our retribution - we've spurned the light of time.

Our children are like diamonds, and ready to receive
such loving care and teaching, their sparkle to achieve.
A shining set of values and a zest to find things out,
and care for other creatures, and concern for all about
this world we treat so badly, will lead them, in their prime,
to the source of our compassion; they'll see the light of time.

So let's have a new beginning, with honesty and truth.
We'll hear the voice of history, and share it with our youth.
We need their range of talents that are there to be employed,
but we also need respect for them so they want to be enjoyed.
We all require an insight, and a reason and a rhyme,
to come back to our senses and regain the light of time.

Bruce Ing

HOLIDAYS AT HENDAYE

The nurses in pink walk on the sand
Purposefully dabbling their toes in the Atlantic.
A break into normality.
Behind them, the high green fence of the hospital
Cuts the grass from the beach.

Between the fence and the breaking sea
People lie worshipping, oiled, flat, unmoving,
Eyes closed, listening to nothing.
Matrons breast the shoreline under parasols,
Men dig happily with bright, minute spades.
Castles, dams, tunnels appear
And disappear with the tide.

Along the sand, far away from the town
And convention, families, friends,
Bare cheeked face with abandon
The creaming surf.
The members of the beach tennis club
Are swinging. A solitary, bronzed
Figure stands with dignity
Watching the waves, wearing
A bright green swimming cap.

While the nurses in pink patrol the shore.

Fran Harris

REFLECTIONS

Things can change from day to day,
What we think and how we play.
Sometimes skies are always blue,
Other times, not knowing what to do.
Days can be quite long and lonely
Wishing for your one and only.
News can be good or bad
Thinking of what you had.
Other days may change your life
Ease your pain and ease your strife.
People you meet and get to know
Even if they only say 'Hello!'
Helps make the world a better place
And put a smile upon your face.

Joyce Hammond

SANTA CLAUS

Tis Christmas again and all are asleep,
so warm and snug in bed,
the little brown heads on the pillows so white,
are dreaming of Santa in red.
No voices are heard on this frosty night,
no voices are heard at all,
but in the silence of the skies,
the snow begins to fall.

Now Jack Frost has come, to paint the boughs,
down lanes all thick with snow
and windows are lit with candlelight,
which casts a gentle glow.
A fairy sits on our Christmas tree,
where she begins to spy,
eight reindeer above the chimney pots,
far in the winter sky.

They come through the snow and fall on our shed,
with one big mighty bump,
I quickly awake, when the doors start to shake
and from my bed do jump.
Old Santa now waves, then points to the sky,
so up to the roof they go,
he quickly drops down our chimney pot
and falls in the room below.

His cheeks are red, as red as his coat,
his beard is white as snow,
he drinks a drop of blackberry wine,
to make his cold face glow.
He sits for awhile, with his belly so round
and munches a large mince pie,
he chuckles and smiles in front of the fire
and makes a cosy sigh.

The stockings are filled, with lots of good things,
a drum, some soldiers and toys,
the elves have read the books he brings,
all chosen for girls and boys.
They work through the year and are busy as bees,
they fill up a Christmas sleigh,
Old Santa has brought ev'ry letter you sent
and notes what you do say.

His reindeer now wait and shiver and shake,
so up the chimney he goes,
he sits on his sleigh in the cold frosty night
and wiggles his freezing toes.
Then off through the skies, like a ship through the foam,
they quickly make their way,
across the country roads, and towns,
before the break of day.

Old Santa now shouts from up in the sky,
his voice is loud and clear,
A Merry Christmas To One And All,
to All A Happy New Year.
Remember the people who need your help,
remember their Christmas Day,
a present will gladden a heart with joy,
in lands so far away.

Tom Clarke

WHERE WE LIVE (YOU AND ME)

We live today in a world of change
Computers, mobile 'phones, dvd's, quite a range
Big macs, e-mails, designer jeans
Internet, fast cars, beyond our means

Life on credit, out goes cash
in the fast lane forever rash
carpe diem, all for now
plastic cards - we know how!

How to live in two thousand and three
consume, 'live the life' you and me
In the West we do all this
a moments thought for those who miss?

Miss this world in the comfort zone
sans car, compact disc, designer telephone;
those who starve and early die
born so low, no piece of pie.

Big pie embraced, we strut our stuff
sometimes caring, but not enough
too distressed for us to face
comforted in our soft rat race.

A race to strive for, gain and win
pipers paid in coins of sin
owt for nowt careerists advise
educated, knowledgeable, but none too wise.

Stop, think, as well as do
of millions poorer than me and you
help with time, a listening ear
give flight, let go to what we fear.

Clive Bowen

DEVIL'S BRIDGE, KIRBY, LONSDALE

Tell me, please and tell me soon,
Who built Devil's Bridge across the Lune.
Who shaped that arch so tall and fair,
Which mason built it with such love and care?

An edifice so very useful,
So strong and yet so beautiful.

And where are those chisels and heavy maul,
That made it possible to build at all?
And the apprentices too, that worked their task,
Supplying the mason with whatever he asked.

Oh bridge so old, or are you still young,
Many centuries will pass until you are done.
You have stood up to rain and hail and snow,
And braced yourself 'gainst storms that blow.

Fair bridge, you are a beauty to behold.
Beauty and strength are yours to hold.
If the devil built you, then I am surprised,
To find he had such beauty, in his eyes.

Albert E Bird

POKIPAN

'Twas on a starboiled aftergrub,
The Gibbleforths came round to gloop.
They dribble-bobbed and poodle-parped
And both of them got up my floop.

Mistress Gibbleforth is fat
And soft and round like bolibols.
Her husband is a hoggle-pig
Who's fond of grils in fal de lols.

My gumptious friend, the Pokipan,
Was fostic sniffing in the wode.
He chanced to meet the Gibbleforths
While on their way to my abode.

He slyly slooped behind the pair,
And hid himself beside a brick.
He piddle-pooped and boggle bopped
And played a most stupendous trick.

The Gibbleforths, they bored me stiff,
They drivelled on about thin air.
And as they jawed they failed to see
The Pokipan upon the stair.

He popped his bag of fostic gum.
A noxious odour spiralled out.
It quite enmeshed the Gibbleforths
And gave them both a gassy clout.

They left! I've never seen them since.
Oh golly bops, my poppled chum,
You saved me from the worstest fate,
But!
I hate your smelly fostic gum!

Lucy Fell

SAD, SAD WORLD

Driving to work on a fine spring day
A little bird across my path did lay
With broken wings:
The juggernauts came crashing overhead,
The little birdie lie there almost dead.
I could not stop, the traffic moved at such a pace,
This is the sad, sad story of the human race:
No time to stop, to think, to care,
With everybody rushing everywhere.

William J Bartram

HELP!

My family decided to visit a store
But I stayed outside in the car.
I felt hot and sticky, phew! What a bore
I could do with a trip to a bar!
Then I suddenly noticed a man and a girl
With a trolley packed up to the top.
The thoughts in my head began to whirl . . .
Had they bought the whole of the shop?
He lifted the boot of a largish saloon
And struggled to put one package in;
He might as well try to jump over the moon
His chances would be just as thin!
He decided to take off all cardboard
To disclose a huge folding table;
Then some large sections of hardboard
And two garden chairs - well known label.
His girlfriend just stood there quite meekly,
I wonder what thoughts filled her head?
She smiled at his efforts so weakly,
I couldn't guess what she had said.
He tried all the board and then the chairs,
Went back to the table again.
I bet he was thinking of saying his prayers
As he studied the how, where and when!
My family came out of the store at this time . . .
The young man was still holding a chair,
I'm certain without intervention sublime . . .
He's still struggling vainly out there!

E Balmain

LITTLE ME

Little me, who could tell,
Life would turn out quite so well,
Who would want to marry me,
Nobody that I could see,
But, you did didn't you?
And I found love, so true,
Happy childhood, for our
Daughter and son,
Life with you is so much fun,
There have been hard times
As well it's true,
But you have me, and I have
All of you,
Now we have our own family tree,
And it's growing rapidly,
Little me, who could tell,
My life would turn out quite so well?

Maureen Arnold

CARPE DIEM

Just leaving now from platform four.
The minutes that have gone before.

The ones you idly threw away
While waiting for a better day
The ones that somehow just slipped by
The ones when you made someone cry
The extra hours you laid in bed
With thoughts of nonsense in your head
The times you said no, not just now
I'll get round to it soon somehow
The ones spent waiting in a queue
The ones who wondered what to do
The hours you slaved to pay the rent
Then can't remember where it went
The ones protecting damaged pride
When you played tough but should have cried
The time spent silent when you should have talked
The times you stayed when you should have walked
The times you should have told the truth
Mis-spent old age and mis-spent youth.

Just departed, platform four
The minutes that have gone before.
Just arriving, platform ten
The minutes you have left to spend.

John Andrews

UNTITLED

'Live and let live'
My dad would say
'Give and forgive'
Not a fad for today
'Water under
The bridge'
My dad would say
'Give and forgive'
Not a fad
For today.

Philip Allen

'ANGING IN THE SHED

Pray, will someone kindly tell me why,
Before I go completely mad,
That when I'm seeking something
I need, really, really bad;
The spike that prizes stones and grit
From limping horses hooves,
Or lengths of iron you join up
For climbing up on roofs,
The rods that click together
To help unblock the drain
Or stuff for round the window
To help keep out the rain.
Gadgets, strange and alien,
Like spronks or bongaloos!
Things from far Australia,
Spare parts for kangaroos,
I bet that when I find one,
No matter how near or far
As I'm going home with it,
I'll meet the one
Whose words will on me jar;
'You really should have asked me,
At least, you might have said,
I've had one of those for ages,
'anging up inside my shed!'

James Allen

A THEORY OF BELIEF

Sanctified blackened milk
Served on silk

A banquet of pain
I need to refrain

From this illusion
And take heed of realities intrusion

It's knocking on the door
Do I open and see more?

Do I open the eye
Or reside in a lie?

It's still beating on the door
Leaving me torn on the floor

Peeping through the keyhole, what a sight
Frozen by it, what a fright

Do I destroy all that mattered
But to do so I'll be shattered

Do I choose an angel
Or change the angle?

Now the seal has been broken
and I have found the unspoken

So why do I seek remission
I guess this is to become a regular tradition.

David C Christopher

STABS IN THE DARK

Some people hazard a guess as to what the future might hold
Those who think they are wise invest in stocks and gold.
There is some common thread, not the world-wide web,
Something more sublime, not ruled by the laws of time.

Perhaps this thread knows nothing of compromise
Even for humanity, an imperfect demise,
Rules by the laws of nature, the laws we have rebuked,
Over natural regulations, humanity has puked.

We are high on our own waste, a toxic brewery in mass production,
Founded at the beginning of the industrial revolution.
The greenhouse carbon cocktail has certainly matured with time
Enhancing violence, the drug with no sense or rhyme.

Are our passions abnormal, blemished by ill-judgement?
Brought on by the toxic-tail of the sometimes sulphur hail.
The planet suffers hourly from extreme torture,
Sulphur burns all over from Belfast to Calcutta.

The planets have no pressure groups to publicise their treatment
They may soon be dependent upon industrial bereavement,
Mass human bereavement my be the next logical step
Can we not change the logic? Adopt a fresh tact.

Tim Frogman

BABY BLISS

At first it seems that life is an abyss,
To bring newborn into a world of want,
To guide the fruits of love plucked from life's font,
To steer the magic bliss of times like this.
Then joys once shared are those without equal,
First steps, then speech, then other wondrous things.
When come to those whose love-heart often sings
They try galore, for more, for love's sequel.

No boredom nor time for parents to wear,
Never-ending, the novel joys abound,
With each blissful day come action and sound
Of life, of child love for them to share.
Faint hearts can never win this wondrous prize,
This bliss that fills abyss of loving lives.

Nick Clifton

DAYDREAMS

If I was only half the girl I'd really like to be,
I'd first hide all my feelings - on show for all to see!

I'd smile serenely when perturbed, and never turn a hair;
I'd raise my eyebrows, look aloof - and show I didn't care.

Instead of blushing furiously . . . I wish I knew a way
that I could kill embarrassment, with witty things to say.

I'd calmly walk into a room, and take my place *in view,*
instead of waiting for a chance to hide inside the loo.

I'd know my outfit looked just great - I'd really 'cut a dash'
I wouldn't have to change *three times . . .* and still have colours clash!

I'd know my face was velvet smooth, my lipstick shade just right,
I'd *never,* ever, find a spot that looked an awful sight.

I thought that age brought confidence, experience of life,
a loving husband, happy home - to feel a *wanted* wife

but maybe if I sit and think, I'll realise my wealth
no confidence, but happiness and most of all, *good health.*

Beryl Clark

OUR RICH LIFE

Some say the world is a frightening place,
Filled with evil and terror, a real disgrace:
Despotic leaders who torture and kill:
Discriminating bigots, removing free will.
Drug trafficking, smuggling, shoplifting;
Bullying and robbery, it's all quite disturbing.
Muggings and rapes, cruel domestic crimes:
There have never been such wicked times.

But nothing's changed. It's always been the same.
Instant global media is to blame
For endless reports of grief and distress.
Virtue and kindness don't make good press.

There's much that is good in the world today:
Moves towards peace, and finding a way
Of redistributing wealth, bringing famine relief.
Diverse religions, harmonised despite belief;
Carers surrendering their own lives daily;
Young people confronting life fairly and squarely:
Tolerant, non-judgmental and prejudice free.
Our life is rich, and as full as we want it to be.

Valerie Catterall

BLACKENED TUNNEL

I'm in a blackened tunnel, not knowing where I'm going,
Where is the light? Where is the hope that is never glowing?
The stress and pressure that I feel,
Will the pain ever heal?
I cannot get out, I'm in too deep,
To recover from this blackened sleep,
I want the things to be back the same,
When I was young the brightness came.
What went wrong with my life?
When I became your lonely wife.
Things went downhill at a rapid rate,
That I've ended up in this state.
I wanna get out, I wanna be free,
From this awful misery.

The things that I want are beyond my reach,
Within my fantasy,
Is there anyone out there that can help me?
I'm feeling sorry for myself that is true,
But after this nightmare of suffering wouldn't you?
For years I have tried to keep things afloat,
With debts and bills, I cannot cope,
Will things ever get better in my life
Or will I always be your lonely wife?

I'd love to have a grand old house,
Fit for a princess, not a mouse,
I'd love to have nice clothes to wear,
Pay my bills without a care,
I'd love to have new of everything,
I'd love to hear Pavarotti sing,

I'd love to have a party for all my friends,
And travel in a Mercedes Benz.

But this is dreaming that won't ever come true,
Back to reality of feeling down and blue,
Where do I go from here on in?
Onwards and upwards that's a grin!

Linda Chapman

DISHARMONY

Among the many reasons for my discontent
Is the lunacy of a modernising government.
Cannot I be the only one who is so annoyed?
The health minister would claim me paranoid.

What, if any achievement, has it made?
None, but to make all people sore afraid,
Lest all their meagre savings shall be seized,
To help keep local council palms well greased.

Glibly politicians speak, seeking to buy votes,
But yet may find they have hit wrong notes.
What a wondrous route to register dissension,
Would be universal electoral mass abstention.

Could that not lead, to but more of the same?
Would this poor scribbler deserve the blame?
More likely for him a post to take, in cabinet.
As proletariats can all too soon, quickly forget.

If so, would such a one as I ban lines poetic,
Apart from mine own tired doggerel frenetic?
For me so to do, would clearly be most unfair,
And rightly damned, along with 'peacefool' Blair.

Perchance to be his deputy might be my lot
To supersede the crass, verbose, Prescott.
Listeners, if any, might achieve their wish,
Of hearing speech spoken in plain English.

Anne Omnibus

OUR WORLD TODAY

In this world of conflict
Always waiting for a war to begin.
We think of peace and happiness,
To fight and kill would be a sin.

for Jesus taught us to love one another
Whether yellow, black or white,
To live together like sister and brother
and never for us to fight.

There must be some other way,
To conquer that evil one.
For every dog has its day.
And God's will, 'will' be done.

Betty Greig

BRIDGE

heart, heart
you are my salvation in the dark
you are my foundation
in a sinking world
you are my life
my girl, my girl
take my hand and lead me on
give me belief when it's all gone
you are my bridge across
all troubled waters
my beloved, only daughter

Steven Gunning

AMERICAN SPACE TRAGEDY

The American spaceship has crashed in the air
It burnt up all the astronauts that were there
Over the Texas land way up in the sky
You could see a trail of light where the astronauts die
They were successful on going in space
And were a credit to the human race
Experiments done they were returning to Earth
To the safety of loved ones to find a safe berth

But something went wrong way up in the sky
And seven of our best astronauts just had to die
Over two miles long was their fiery trail
From the land in Texas you could see it without fail
Pieces of it fell down on the motorway
Missing cars that were travelling to town on their way
Pieces were blackened where they had caught alight
This accident happened in the day not the night

For over two hundred miles they were spread
No sight of course of the seven dead
Their bodies were ash spread over the land
Blown to the four corners of their homeland
They will be remembered for many years
By the families left behind who now shed tears
Let us hope their journey was not all in vain
And let's hope those poor astronauts did not die in pain

Jocky

MOTHER NATURE

Her flamboyant style, and flowing hair,
She drifts along, doesn't seem to care,
Where she goes, no one knows.
She just turns up, in colourful clothes,
Skirts a swirling, a jaunty walk,
She never stops, she never talks.

A lady of mystery, but full of grace,
Sometimes at a more leisurely pace,
Sometimes cold, warm or hot,
This lady has the lot.
With icy fingers, eyes ice blue
Gives one the shivers through and through.

Just like the seasons, all the four,
Cold, warmth, heat, then cool once more.
How she does it, we are not quite sure.
She does to the rich, and to the poor,
Whether you're Catholic, Protestant or a Quaker,
We all bow down to Mother Nature.

Don Friar

SHE'S CALLING FROM WITHIN

The wild and dark tempestuous sea
Insists she has to talk to me
I don't know what she wants to say
But know I feel I have to stay

She's wild and yet she can be calm
A sea that could not do one harm
Alas her moods change like the wind
Her promises she must rescind

She calls and tempts us from within
She beckons us to 'come on in'
And then her mood swings, like a child
One moment charming, then so wild

Her undertow pulls left and right
She swirls and eddies, you may fight
But she's so strong, you lose your feet
And fall on cushioned sand so sweet

She's spoken to you, let's take care
She's taught you how to be aware
Be careful now, there's others who
Won't be so kind or gentle, so

Beware of what you perceive to be
A dark or calm nonentity
Because, I think, you'll surely find
The hidden mystique of mankind

Sue Elle

TWO PAINTINGS

His ancient faith was simple and sincere.
The works communicate serenity.
Whether or not he invented oil painting,
and whatever the relative merits of Hubert,
the elder brother, it's neither here nor there.
Each canvas glows with faith's illumination.

In Bruges' Groeninge, the dough-faced Canon,
Jordis van der Paele, kneels at the Virgin's feet,
a stalwart burgher, one of the bourgeoisie, unfit,
larding spirituality with sensuality.
Black iron spectacles bookmark his holy missal,
his ample surplice testimony to his appetites.

Meticulous observation, miraculously rendered:
rich stuffs, brocade with filigree, intricate chain mail,
smooth, marble columns, oriental carpet's nap,
jewelled cope and crosier, human flesh -
he was a navigator, Columbus of the visible world,
who, in his explorations, sacramentalized.

Now take the Brussels train one stop to Ghent
and make your way to the Cathedral, there to kneel
before the altarpiece. Adam and Eve stand naked,
life-sized, dispossessed of Eden and all its bounty,
stretching beyond the horizon, fifty miles away,
beyond each dewdrop trembling in each buttercup.

The artist's eye, both telescope and microscope,
is as the eye of God, its scrutiny self-transcending.
The natural and mystical co-exist. They synthesise,
harmoniously. His every gout of pigment's charged with faith.
His world's a storehouse, inexhaustible, serene.
If God could paint, this is how He would paint.

Norman Bissett

SLEEP SABOTAGE

No night as long as a night without sleep
Nothing more difficult than cheerful thoughts to keep
No bedside clock looked at more times in a night
Welcome would be a noisy party or fight

Comforting thoughts are soon pushed aside
When your mind is obsessed by fears you can't hide
Are you really as well as you appear to be?
Will a serious illness strike suddenly?

Is that smoke you can smell and if you open the door
Will flames engulf with a mighty roar?
Impending panic threatens and will not abate
Until you stop thinking thoughts that you hate

Try as you will you soon discover
One fear overcome is replaced by another
You're really in trouble when you do
Start to believe they will come true

Joyce Atkinson

A LITTLE HUMOUR

It was just a little humour
Just a little joke
But it got a little out of hand
And ended up in smoke.

It was just a little humour
To get us all to laugh
But it has really gone wrong
And here we are looking and feeling daft.

It was just a little humour
So we must take more care
And make sure in the future
Someone is always there.

Keith L Powell

KNOW EACH OTHER

A community where we can walk safely down the street,
To greet the people that we meet,
Good morning, how are you?
A pleasant way to start the day.
To visit the shops, to meet with friends,
Just to buy some odds and ends.
A birthday present, a Christmas gift.
A new shopping centre a stereotype,
All new town centres look alike.
We search for bargains, for cheaper food,
A big family can be a hungry brood.
And late relax in the community club,
And discuss the things you want to do.
Perhaps hire a disco some weekends,
Plan some outings for the coming months.
Having a social drink and playing darts,
Even the kids having fun can take part.
A genial atmosphere as it should be,
Street parties, barbecues, having fun,
All friends in the street, everyone.
Perhaps more towns could be the same,
Any size community can get together,
And create days of absolute pleasure.
Some day we will have to take a stand,
Join forces make this a happy land.
Let's not separate black and white,
Let's all sleep safe at night.

Tom Usher

ANGUISH

My eldest daughter
Would love a child
She'd make a good mother
And that's been mild.

It makes her sad
But if she had
The wealth
It would help

Fostering she could not take
Mainly for her own sake
It would break her heart so
When they had to go

Adoption is the next best thing
That would perhaps make her sing
A lot of red tape involved
Before it could be resolved

Ideally she would have her own
If only she could get a loan
IVF is very expensive
And the treatment would be extensive

I just hope
Her dreams come true
She will cope
With a glass of brew.

Pat Hunter

SAVING THE PLANET

Recycle, recycle, recycle or so they say we must,
  Or else the earth's crust will turn to infertile dust.
So off we drive in our cars every Sunday morn,
  In our efforts to save the planet for a generation as yet unborn.
To hurl our empty bottles, clear, brown or green,
  Into the big bin next to the parking ticket machine.

Then into the supermarket we go, list in hand,
  To buy tins and packets that scarce resemble the fruits of the land.
The way nature intended us to live we seem to have forgot,
  So wrapped up are we in progress, technology and improving our lot.
So headlong into an artificial future we plunge, no time to pause
  And listen to those who make the Earth's well being their
                                        heartfelt cause.
It's all right! We can save the Earth for the generation as yet unborn,
  As long as we recycle our bottles every Sunday morn.

Fiona Louise Watson

TIME

It's a pity time goes flying by
You often hear people give a sigh
And wish they had time to enjoy
The pastimes in which they themselves employ
If only we had time to stop and stand
And think about the things we've planned
Whatever we do, we always have a shock
When we look at that annoying clock
The seconds, minutes and hours go so fast
As the best times go rushing past
All the things you plan to do
Even though they are exciting but few
Seem hardly to come before they go
Why this happens you don't really know
But it all is the fault of one thing
'Time', the end to all things will bring
So let's make the best of the things we enjoy most
Because time is always there like a horrible ghost
So next time you do something really good
Forget about time like you really should
And think and enjoy it as best you can
And ignore the greatest enemy of man.

Christine Mitchell

FRIEND ON DRUGS

Why destroy what is truly yours?
Am I the only one that can see?
A piece of leather - a simple treasure
A friendship that you gave to me

But now you have changed, all the hurt and the hate
That you think that the world throws at you
You perceive in your mind that the world is unkind
So what life are you now turning to?

The mutual love of the world that you met
It was yours in the palm of your hand
But you shied away, less believing each day
To the answer you don't understand

Why do you hide in a tomb of deceit?
Do you really believe what you feel?
A temporary high as your life rushes by
And a way of avoiding what's real

Dawn Wylie

ULTIMATE AIM

I sleep with the light on and dream of you,
the way you walk and everything else you do,
the way I feel for you words can't explain,
and when I'm alone it drives me insane,
you're the reason that I'm alive,
if you were not here I'd honestly die,
you lift up my days and light up my nights,
just for you the whole world I'd fight,
by your side that's where I'd love to be,
all alone together just you and me,
us to be together is my ultimate aim,
we'd make mad passionate love again and again.

Louise Davies

THE RACE

Why must my bum fart
To the rhythm of my heart
Whilst I'm waiting for the start

Hold on tight
I see the green light
Let us take flight

Oh s**t! Oh dear!
We're bringing up the rear
But I see a racing line that's clear

Don't get in a flap, another lap
We've almost closed the gap
Another lap, another lap

And now I see the winning line
I know the race is mine
Three cheers. Where is the fizzy wine?

Clare Todd

TRUE FRIENDSHIP

The joy of friendship is always there
For you and me and all to share
As we go through life from the very start
True friendships are formed and all play a part
They shape our lives with love and care
And when times are hard true friendship is there
To be without friends would be very sad
They help us to live and be happy and glad
We see bonds of friendship in everyday life
And joy and love also sadness and strife
As we look at the world in which we live
We all have the need and pleasure to give
Some friends are with us for all time to be
Making the world better for you and me
One of the greatest gifts from above
Is really true friendship given with love

Joyce Stokes

WHEN YOUR SHIP COMES IN

If you feel that you're 'hard done by'
And your 'Good Times' should begin,
With a cargo of 'Good Fortune'
When your ship comes in.

Take the time to look around you
Counting wheelchairs, 'special' schools,
the blind, the deaf
And those who cannot walk.
The mentally disabled,
The starving child abroad
And then, there are the folk who cannot talk.

Reflect upon these things, and then,
Should you find, you're not in line,
You will see, when looking once again
Your ship's been in, all the time.

Leslie Frank Checkley

T' NEW YEAR

T'day's start o'fresh new year
It's goin' t' be a good un
I've got some resolutions 'ere
I'm sure I can achieve one of 'em.

Mi first un is a daily walk
T' th' end o' road 'n' back.
Eawr dog 'Boris' can cum too
But thowt makes me feel whacked.

I'm stoppin' eatin' chocolate 'n' sweets
I mean not every day.
I'm gonna survive on two rations a week
Instead o' three times a day.

Mi next un is t' be more nice t' folk
When I'm feelin' poorly myself.
'N' say, "ow are yer,' 'nd "ave a nice day'
When I want t' crawl 'n' hide under a shelf.

There's a thowt t' drink more water
Eight glass I'll drink, four lots times two.
I'll start wi' them great giant tumblers
If not, then, eight egg cups will do!

'N' if I canna manage all or any o'these
Be patient and please understand.
Cos resolutions aren't always fer keepin'
But makin' 'em's really quite grand!

Mandy M McKee

I Am Waiting

I'm up early an appointment you see,
Visit to hospital and it's foggy,
Miles from home, traffic galore,
Not a good day that's for sure,
I'm quiet and subdued,
What will doc tell me, what be the news?
After what seems like hours,
Travelling I'm actually there,
People around, not any chairs,
I'm waiting, I'm waiting and nothing can I do,
I'm stuck in a waiting room,
Dismal too,
The place looks tidy and clean at glance,
A good thing although they could enhance,
A better system a better way,
To prevent hours of waiting on appointment day,
It's very boring sitting around,
Gloom on people's faces and frown,
No one is friendly, they're too engrossed,
Hoping the staff have not lost their notes,
Yes they called my name at last,
Not just yet, not so fast,
Another room, another wait,
By this time I had a headache,
So I've just one message to say to you,
Don't take ill whatever you do.

Carol Boneham

I'M ON MY OWN

Now that you're gone,
I'm on my own,
Wondering when you're coming home,
How does this have to be,
Are you coming back to me?
We will always be,
For eternity,
I can't stop thinking about you,
There's something about you,
You're true to me,
Why can't you see,
You're my number one.

Kirsty Wing

THE YOUNG OF TODAY

The youth of today, they make me so sad,
They treat their young bodies, with such disregard.
They ignore good advice, on exercise and fresh air
They think this is for olds, who have no other care.
When out with their mates, they try acting so cool,
With a big cigarette as their number one tool,
The warning on the packet, they take no heed,
Warnings like these sure we have no need
The time comes along and discos are the call,
Or maybe a dance or a fancy dress ball.
This is as it should be there is no doubt at all,
But why oh why must they drink alcohol?
When you're young and you're free and your body is healthy,
With today's opportunities the world is your oyster.
Alcohol is a drug and let no one say other
And drugs are addictive and cause so much bother,
So young people listen,
To advice you've been given,
Treat your own body as a fine place to live in.

Margaret McIlwaine

BIRTHDAYS

Birthdays are special when you're a child
You get lots of presents and play and eat until you're tired

Birthdays are special when you're in your teens
Sleepovers and outings and growing up's what it means

Birthdays are special as you come of age
Clubbing and parties and earning a wage

Birthdays are special as the next 0's pass by
You keep your age quiet - it might make you cry

Birthdays are special as you start to mature
Time to relax and rest from a chore

But when you reach old age
And the years have racked up
You'll go back to your childhood
And drink from a spout on a cup

Jill Corkish

Untitled

Hello, my name is Jenny and I'm living on the streets
You pretend that you don't know me but you do
You've seen me many times before, in better times than this
At least they were for me but not for you

You think I'm just another one, another worthless case
A girl who's thrown away her chance at life
Why should I have a second try? I messed up on the first
Besides I'll only get into some strife

I haven't learned my lesson, I really quite enjoy
Being treated as an animal would be
The people supposed to find me jobs have asked me please to leave
No doubt because I smell, but can you see?

I've never tried to start again because it wouldn't work
My hope has finally been quite put out
It'll take me quite a while to ever trust someone again
Because of things that you don't know about

The first time that I slept here on a cold and stony floor,
In the back street of your favourite local town
Was the last time I remember having life of any sort
And now that life has died, is not around

I'm not an alcoholic though I almost wish I was
Even drugs would take some of the pain away
All I need is someone there to pick me up again
To give me a new life, not in the way

Hello my name is Jenny and I'm living on the streets
I know I cannot be helped just by you
But if I ruled the world I know exactly what I'd change
I'd change the life of me, and so should you.

Jenny Mill

AWAKENING

I hear the words crashing into mind
It was weird that I could be so blind
I didn't listen before it seems
Too busy with my inner dreams.
Attention now I can surely give
Before they go I'll let them live
Alter my view of all around
Allow me to hear the hidden sound
Of my self-conscious sure as it is
And not just the noise of a background fizz.
If they were right then I'll agree
So maybe then you'll let me be
It's more important that I think for myself
And possibly acquire some little wealth
For a dreamer is usually pretty poor
And people may think one pretty dour
Then words strung together and made to rhyme
Are easy to follow and enter fine
So rather than just hear, I listen too
And I comment with words quite new
Not what I heard through my ears
Within my head the answer rears
I speak out loud, vibrate the air
Repeat the words if I dare
If everything stays fair
I'll care.

Robert McGarry

SAILING

Sailing on a calm blue sea on a bright hot summer's day
Seagulls flying overhead porpoises at play
Pleasure suddenly turns to fright as the waves begin to swell
The wind whips through the canvasses the boats tossed like a shell
All the hatches are battened as we head towards the shore
The waves are getting larger and the wind is now a roar
We ride the waves the wind and the spray
Our sails now tattered and torn
But look the sky is brightening like the hour before dawn
Then as quickly as it came the storm has passed us by
Now we're sailing on a calm blue sea
Under a clear blue sky

Christopher F Morris

THE EVENING CLASS

Autumn evening wild and windy, just past six, the end of day,
smiling now our city worker dons her coat at close of play.
Tired her eyes from cold computing blinking in the fading daylight
weary sighs, relief is coming. 'Pint of beer?' Perhaps I might.

Time is short so to the tube train, bent umbrella fights the fine rain
push and shove through ticket barriers,
down to hell with countless sinners,
garlic breath and curry dinners, bulging briefcase, Harrods carriers.

Oh the pain of our commuter pressed up tight against a stranger!
Traffic's bad, it's such a pity. Brimming bowels of the city!
Wished she'd driven arriving later, dodging cars and courting danger.
Warm, stale air smells thick and sickly, noses wrinkle, tempers prickly,
angry ant steam, bright lit tunnel, busy, buzzing through its funnel,
cranky trains and crammed commuters, arguments, apple computers
muttering mantras, stress reducers
clutching tight on slippery stairwell paperbacks by Auden, Orwell.

Heart with alcohol a fluttering, caffeine-fuelled muscles pumping,
fast she climbs the escalator, deftly dodged perambulator,
fights her way through bodies bumping, head and heart both
madly thumping
But it's worth it! Such a pleasure, stimulation now awaits her,
hers to read, to write, to listen, ruminate on life's condition.
Out onto the bustling Broadway, Hammersmith and Chiswick hustle,
London's usual mad tussle. Keats and Byron. Hemmingway.

Past the banks and past the Lyric, past the ugly office civic
words of poets, rhyming, singing, Shakespeare's sonnets, hearts
for ringing
Oh how wonderful the yearning! Scent the flower of our learning
freedom from the daily grind, free to exercise her mind,
discover classics, education, poems for her delectation,
English language exploration, poultice for life's mutilation, solace,
soul regeneration.
Doing in a world of watching, risk revealing her creations.

Turn off King Street, Macbeth Centre, where's the courage God has lent her?

Red brick school that someone rich built, children's ghosts, class wars and old guilt

Now it's hers to chorus Chaucer, dreams by Blake awaken, thrill her.

Seven o'clock join fellow students, writing, drawing, painting glass.

Is her nervousness transparent? Is her ignorance apparent?

Will they spot she lacks the talent?

Time for fun to trounce her shyness. Time to start her poetry class.

Joy Lewis

THE MERMAID AND THE TROUBADOUR

You walked the beach one morning as the sun's rays first appeared.
A wind and wave creation, to my mind, solar geared.
You stare to the horizon, while waves queued to kiss your feet,
Gulls dance their aerial ballet, wheel and then retreat.

Your small and childlike footprints trail behind you as you pass,
Daring me to follow where you lead and take a change.
In past lives, I was Icarus, a moth seared in life's heat
But still, I am drawn to you though it may mean defeat.

If you will be my mermaid I'll be your troubadour
And we'll sing and dance our way along the shore.

Your warmth is overwhelming but I follow where you go.
The sun renews our vigour so no tiredness we show.
My wings stay strong, no damage done; I've strength to fly away.
Your laugh, it soothes and gentles me. So easy now to stay.

Now night it gathers round us as a sax it far off plays,
Time has flown so quickly while suspended in your gaze.
We build a fire to warm us while our souls are lit, by fires
Sparked by our conversation flowing freely through the hours

If you will be my mermaid I'll be your troubadour
And we'll sing and dance our way along the shore.

Bright morning follows night sure as the sun pursues the moon
To find us lively, animated resting near a dune.
Conversation has not ended and our dance not half begun
So we spark and dance the day away and greet the morning sun.

If you will be my mermaid I'll be your troubadour
And we'll sing and dance our way along the shore.

Patrick Lyseight

A SPIDER'S TALE

I sat nice and cosy in the corner of the shelf
Amongst the books and ornaments all by myself,
When suddenly a loud noise came into the room
Spinning and whirring making my heart boom.

The owner of the household was doing all her chores
I thought I best be on my guard, the noise began to soar.
The cleaner she was using came near to the place . . .
The corner I was hiding in, so I edged back in haste.

Soon the noise abated, a new sound reached my ears,
The smell and hiss of polish as it was squirted near.
I thought . . . this is the time for me to leave my nice and cosy place
Or I'll be coated with this spray right into my face.

As suddenly as I appeared there was a piercing scream
The lady shrieked and howled and yelled
It was like a living dream.

Why was she so frightencd of a small eight legged thing?
It was I who should be scared to death making my ears ring.
I am just a spider who likes to hide away
Best take more care in future or I might not see another day.

Jean Marguerite Dangerfield

THE TURN OF THE CARD

First you are here
Then you are not,
The time in-between
Is all you have got.
Health, wealth, love or hate,
The turn of the card
Decides your fate.
Fame, shame or neither one
Just born under a star
That never shone.
Prince of the realm
Or cog in the wheel,
The turn of the card
And that's the deal.

Beryl Powles

ESSENTIAL AND PRECIOUS
(Nulli Secundus - second to none)

As a small child loves sweets, I love you.
As I think of you now I can cry.
You were always, so very proud of me.
Although often, I ask myself why.
You were there through all of my growing.
In the background your presence so strong.
You were keen to reward me for good things.
Your glance let me know of the wrong.
You were ever my faithful protector.
Firm in action, gentle in thought.
Your responses were truly amazing.
What you gave me can never be bought.
Of your love, I never was doubtful.
Oh, your trust it stretched out for miles.
How I wish I could chat with you now Dad!
How I long for just one of your smiles!

Christine Frederick

EDUCATION PLUS

When my folk sent me to college,
I had no thought of carnal knowledge;
Their intention was for me to learn to spell:
That with languages and Euclid,
Although they thought me stupid,
I got along reasonably well.

After several weeks tuition,
I discovered that my mission,
Was to meet and make love to Mary Jane,
The daughter of the head,
Who every night she went to bed,
Waved to me and called me by the name.

One night she stood in wait,
At the head's back garden gate,
As I nonchalantly walked by:
She grabbed me by the arm,
Turning on the charm,
Grabbing at my new school tie;
She pulled me into the hall,
And said, 'Let's have a ball,
'Ma and Pa are out you see.'

I really felt ecstatic,
As she led me to the attic,
What was in store for me?
She opened up the door,
And there upon the floor
Was the finest toy train set
You ever did see!

Lionel J Nokes

THE TIES THAT BIND

(Dedicated to my sister, my best friend)

One lives here, one lives there
One is dark, one is fair
Two different people you never would see
But tied by a bond as deep as the sea

One is a traveller, one stays at home
One is restless, one cannot roam
Two different lives and paths were took
But bound together like leaves of a book

One is angry, one is calm
One sees no danger, one can see harm
Two different outlooks on life they both see
But united together as strong as can be

One is weak, one is strong
One is content, one don't belong
Two different feelings may rule their heart
But together they're whole and unsettled apart

One never phones, one never writes
Both know it's wrong and it's never alright
Two busy lives that stand in their way
But the ties that bind sisters, forever will stay.

Jo-Ann Waldron-Hall

MAMMO

I miss you more every day
I love you more than words can say
I miss you so much
I miss your loving touch
I miss your laugh
I remember you smile
Even though I haven't seen you for a while
My heart feels like it's breaking
My make-up feels like it's flaking
But your smile will always stay
And I will love you till my dying day.

Carlie Morgans (16)

GOODBYE

Suddenly he has gone, without a goodbye
And I loved him so.
I thought he was coming home again!
Still looking handsome, I held his hand
One cannot escape the distress that follows great happiness
No one to talk to, in my arms an empty space
And in my heart the same
I stand by my window looking out on life
A friendly neighbour, will give me a wave, as she passed by
I miss you so, I sit down with a sigh
The happy years that have passed
Does not prepare you for this abject loneliness
And the great silence, now that you have gone
Goodbye my love.

B Green